MAR 0 6 2017

United States Regions

Northeast and Metropolitan Regions

Nancy Allen

R🌐urke
Educational Media

rourkeeducationalmedia.com

Scan for Related Titles
and Teacher Resources

Before Reading:

Building Academic Vocabulary and Background Knowledge

Before reading a book, it is important to tap into what your child or students already know about the topic. This will help them develop their vocabulary, increase their reading comprehension, and make connections across the curriculum.

1. *Look at the cover of the book. What will this book be about?*
2. *What do you already know about the topic?*
3. *Let's study the Table of Contents. What will you learn about in the book's chapters?*
4. *What would you like to learn about this topic? Do you think you might learn about it from this book? Why or why not?*
5. *Use a reading journal to write about your knowledge of this topic. Record what you already know about the topic and what you hope to learn about the topic.*
6. *Read the book.*
7. *In your reading journal, record what you learned about the topic and your response to the book.*
8. *After reading the book complete the activities below.*

Content Area Vocabulary
Read the list. What do these words mean?

borders
colonies
colonists
habitats
hibernation
melting pot
metropolitan
migrating
settlement
tourists

After Reading:

Comprehension and Extension Activity

After reading the book, work on the following questions with your child or students in order to check their level of reading comprehension and content mastery.

1. *Why does Washington, D.C. have many government workers? (Asking questions)*
2. *New York is considered a melting pot because of all the different cultures and people that live there. What does the term melting pot imply about immigrants in New York? (Inferring)*
3. *How are the natural resources found in the Northeast region used? (Summarize)*
4. *What are some things people do for fun in the Northeast and Metropolitan regions? (Summarize)*
5. *Explain how the Northeast and Metropolitan regions are rich in U.S. history. (Summarize)*

Extension Activity

Think about all the information you read about the Northeast and Metropolitan regions. Create a travel brochure for the U.S. Tourism Department by addressing reasons people should visit these regions. Be sure to include things people can do for entertainment, facts, weather, and a map vertex on a separate sheet of paper. Give your coordinates to a partner to see if they can create the same polygon using only your coordinates.

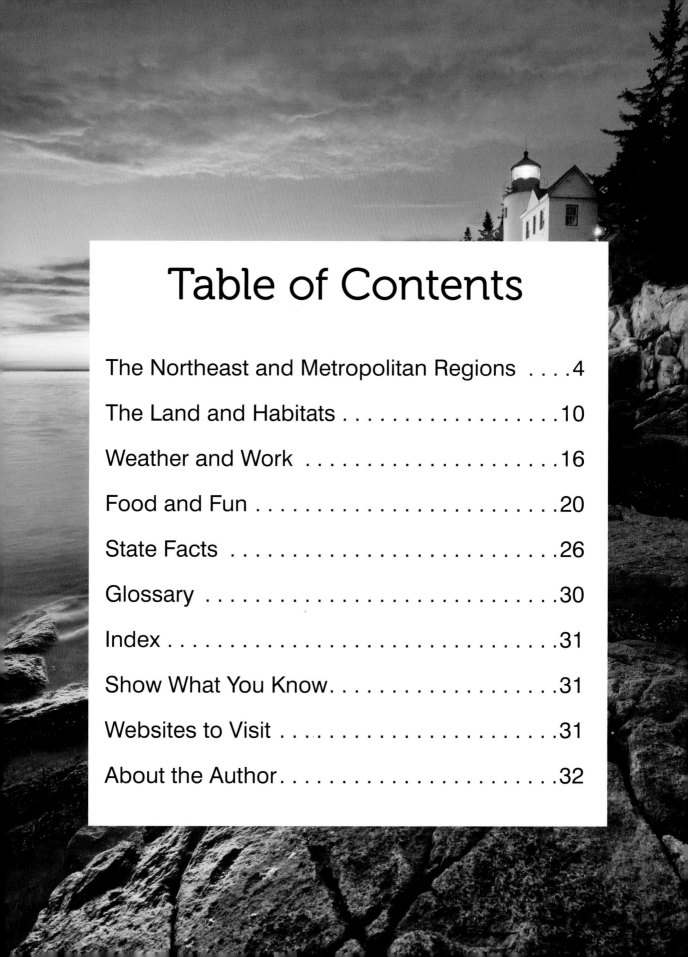

Table of Contents

The Northeast and Metropolitan Regions

In size, the Northeast and **Metropolitan** regions of the United States are small. But in history, they are big.

The Northeast region lies between the Atlantic Ocean on the east and the Great Lakes on the west. Canada **borders** on the north. The Metropolitan region borders on the south. The Northeast states are Maine, Vermont, New Hampshire, New York, Massachusetts, and Rhode Island.

13 Original Colonies

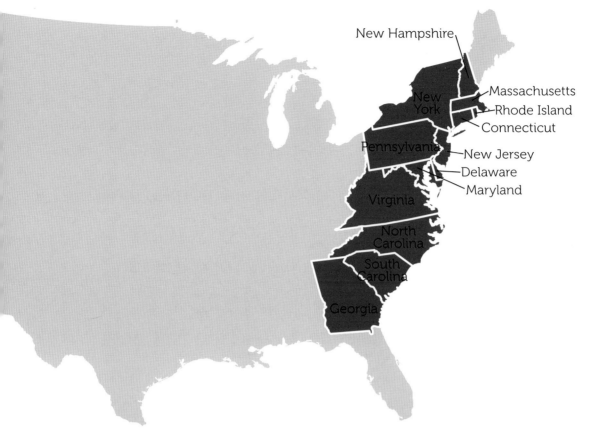

New Hampshire

Massachusetts

Rhode Island

Connecticut

New York

New Jersey

Pennsylvania

Delaware

Maryland

Virginia

North Carolina

South Carolina

Georgia

*The Northeast is the oldest region of the United States. Many of the states began as **colonies** in the 1600s.*

The Metropolitan region lies on the east coast of the United States, just below the Northeast region. The Metropolitan region is identified by the many major cities that fill this small region.

Metropolitan states are Delaware, Maryland, New Jersey, Connecticut, and Washington, D.C. Parts of New York and Pennsylvania make up the Metropolitan region as well.

The Northeast and Metropolitan regions have some of the largest U.S. cities, including New York, Boston, Philadelphia, Baltimore, and Washington, D.C.

Baltimore had the first street lights and the first post office system in the U.S. Boston built the first U.S. library. New York City was the U.S. capital from 1789 to 1790. These cities have helped make America great.

U.S. lawmakers met at Federal Hall in New York City before the capital was moved to Washington, D.C.

The White House

Washington, D.C. is the capital city of the United States. The city is not part of any state. Washington, D.C. was built to be the seat of government for the United States.

The White House and Capitol Building are located in Washington, D.C. U.S. laws are made in the Capitol Building.

U.S. Capitol

Native Americans were the first people to live in these regions. They have lived there for thousands of years.

In 1620, Pilgrims sailed from England. They landed on the coast of Massachusetts. The Pilgrims settled in Plymouth and formed a **settlement** named Plymouth Plantation. It was one of the earliest settlements in the New World. Native Americans taught the Pilgrims how to fish, hunt, and grow corn.

In 1775, America was made up of 13 colonies. The colonies were ruled by Great Britain. They wanted to make their own laws. That year, the **colonists** began fighting Great Britain in the Revolutionary War. The colonists won the war in 1793. They named their country the United States of America.

The Pilgrims had the first Thanksgiving in 1621. They gathered their crops and invited the Native Americans to eat with them. The Native Americans brought deer, and the two groups shared the meal.

The Land and Habitats

The Northeast region has wide valleys, rolling hills, coasts, islands, and mountains. The Appalachian Mountains are the oldest mountains in the United States. They are a group of mountain ranges that run along the entire eastern United States. The Catskill Mountains are in New York, the Green Mountains are in Vermont, and the White Mountains are in New Hampshire. Cadillac Mountain in Maine is the highest peak on the Atlantic Coast. It is the first place the Sun rises each day in the United States.

The longest hiking trail in the world is the Appalachian Trail. The 2,180 mile (3,508 kilometer) trail begins in Maine and ends in Georgia. Each year, about 2,000 people hike the Appalachian Trail from beginning to end. It takes a hiker about 2 million steps to complete the trail.

Rocky coastlines characterize the Northeast region. Much of Maine's coast has jagged rocks and cliffs.

The Metropolitan region has hills covered in forests, wetlands, flat land, rivers, lakes, and coasts. The states in this region have islands along the Atlantic Ocean.

Unlike the rocky coasts of Maine, the Metropolitan region contains more sandy beaches. Maryland and New Jersey have miles of flat, sandy coastlines.

These beaches and shores are **habitats** for sea turtles, horseshoe crabs, and other sea life. The rivers and creeks contain beavers building dams. The forests are home to deer, bear, moose, muskrats, and wild turkeys.

Delaware Bay has more horseshoe crabs than any other place in the world. The area is a habitat to more than 400 kinds of birds. Some are **migrating** birds.

Horseshoe Crab

These regions have many lighthouses. One of the best known lighthouses is in West Quoddy Head, Maine. It is located at the eastern-most point of the United States.

13

Small towns and large cities are located in the Metropolitan region. New York City is the largest U.S. city and a major trade center for the world. Banking, television shows and movies, publishing, and shipping are big businesses.

People from around the world have come to the Metropolitan region's cities to live and work. They came from many different places in the world. The region became known as a **melting pot**.

New Jersey is the only state in which all its counties are metropolitan areas. About 90 percent of its people live in towns and cities.

New York City is home to more than 8 million people. Many work in tall buildings, called skyscrapers.

Weather and Work

These regions have long, cold winters with many snowstorms. One type of storm is called a northeaster. A northeaster can drop more than one foot (30.5 centimeters) of snow. The northern part of the Northeast gets over 100 inches (2.5 meters) of snow each year.

All the states in these regions have four seasons. Spring **tourists** should take a raincoat, just in case you get caught in a sudden springtime rain.

Summers are warm, but short. The average temperature in summer is 80–85° Fahrenheit (26–29° Celsius). The nighttime air is cooler in the mountains and along the coast.

In cold, snowy weather, some animals go into a deep sleep, called **hibernation**. *Bears hibernate up to 100 days.*

The Northeast and Metropolitan regions may be small, but they have big businesses. The Northeast's forests are a good source of wood, which is used to make paper and furniture. Sugar maple trees grow in these regions as well. They produce sap that is boiled and made into maple syrup. The regions' rich soil grows apples, pears, and flowers. Cranberries grow in the sandy, wet soil.

Granite and marble are mined from the area's rock quarries. The stone is used in buildings. Factories produce iron, glass, and steel. Chemicals are used in shampoo, paints, and medicines.

In the Washington, D.C. area, many people work for the U.S. government.

Massachusetts is called the Cranberry Capital. The state produces about 2 million barrels of cranberries each year.

Food and Fun

People live close to the Atlantic Ocean, so they eat a lot of seafood. Clam chowder, crab cakes, and lobster are popular foods.

Locally tapped maple syrup is made into candy and cakes. And fresh-farmed blueberries and grapes are sweet treats. The region's flat land is used for growing apples and dairy farming. Dairy products, such as ice cream and cheese, are also popular.

Baked beans were a favorite food among early settlers in Massachusetts. The food became popular in Boston, earning it the nickname, Beantown.

People living in the Northeast region buy the most ice cream. They have been eating the sweet treat since colonists first came to America.

About 90 percent of U.S. lobsters are caught off the coast of Maine. That's 40 million pounds of lobster each year.

People use snow and ice for sports. They ski down and around mountains. Some skate on frozen lakes. Others go snowboarding, snowshoeing, snow tubing, and dog sledding. They eat the white stuff, too.

Snow Ice Cream Recipe

Ingredients:

8 cups clean, freshly fallen snow

1 can sweetened condensed milk

1/2 teaspoon vanilla extract

Directions:

Place snow in a large bowl. Pour condensed milk over the snow.

Add vanilla extract and mix well.

Over the course of one month, residents of Bethel, Maine built a snow woman measuring 122 feet 1 inch (37.21 meters) tall. They completed their work on February 26, 2008.

Rochester, New York is the snowiest large city in the United States. Rochester gets about 94 inches (2.3 meters) of snow each year.

23

Car racing is popular in the Northeast. Horse racing, football, baseball, hockey, and basketball are other sports people enjoy. Water sports, such as swimming, skiing, and sailing, are fun in the summer.

The Boston Marathon is the oldest footrace in the United States. It began in 1897. The U.S. Open is a tennis tournament held in New York City each year. New York is also home to the Belmont Stakes, a horse race.

The Northeast and Metropolitan regions are home to a great variety of foods, activities, and businesses. The people of these regions help make the United States a great country.

State Facts Sheet

Maine

Motto: I Direct.

Nickname: Pine Tree State

Capital: Augusta

Known for: Lobsters, Lighthouses, Beautiful Coasts, and over 2,000 islands

Fun Fact: Maine grows 99 percent of the blueberries in the United States.

Vermont

Motto: Freedom and Unity.

Nickname: The Green Mountain State

Capital: Montpelier

Known for: Maple Syrup, Lakes, Forests, Covered Bridges, Skiing, and Mountains

Fun Fact: Ben & Jerry's ice cream started in Burlington in 1978.

New Hampshire

Motto: Live Free or Die.

Nickname: Granite State

Capital: Concord

Known for: Maple Syrup, Granite, Lakes, and Beaches

Fun Fact: New Hampshire opened the first U.S. public library.

New York

Motto: Excelsior, which means "Ever Upward."

Nickname: Empire State

Capital: Albany

Known for: Banking, Skyscrapers, and Forests

Fun Fact: New York City was the first capital of the United States. George Washington took his oath as president there in 1789.

Massachusetts

Motto: By the Sword We Seek Peace, but Peace Only Under Liberty.

Nickname: Bay State

Capital: Boston

Known for: Seafood, Cranberries, and Machinery

Fun Fact: Massachusetts was the home of John Chapman, a pioneer known as Johnny Appleseed.

Rhode Island

Motto: Hope.

Nickname: The Ocean State

Capital: Providence

Known for: Making Silverware and Jewelry

Fun Fact: Rhode Island is the smallest state.

New Jersey

Motto: Liberty and Prosperity.

Nickname: The Garden State

Capital: Trenton

Known for: Tomatoes, Agriculture, and Drug Companies

Fun Fact: Water surrounds New Jersey, except for about 40 miles (64.4 kilometers) along the New York border.

Delaware

Motto: Liberty and Independence.

Nickname: First State

Capital: Dover

Known for: Poultry, Soybeans, Rubber, and Plastics

Fun Fact: Delaware Bay has more horseshoe crabs than any other area in the world.

Maryland

Motto: Strong Deeds, Gentle Words.

Nickname: Old Line State

Capital: Annapolis

Known for: Wild ponies that live on islands off the Maryland coast

Fun Fact: Boston Common became the first U.S. public park in 1634.

Connecticut

Motto: He Who Transplanted
  Still Sustains.
Nickname: Constitution State
Capital: Hartford
Known for: Oysters, Whales, Chemicals,
  Computers, Aircraft Manufacturing
Fun Fact: Connecticut Valley has the
  most dinosaur tracks in the world.

Washington, D.C.

Motto: Justice For All.
Became the capital of the United States
  July 1, 1800.
Known for: It is the seat of the
  U.S. government, and home to the
  U.S. president.
Fun Fact: Washington, D.C. is not a state
  and is not part of any state.

Glossary

borders (BOR-durs): dividing lines between two countries or states

colonies (KAH-luh-neez): a place that has been settled by people from another country and is ruled by that country

colonists (KAH-luh-nistz): a settler or inhabitant of a colony

habitats (HAB-i-tats): places where animals or plants live

hibernation (HYE-bur-NAY-shun): to spend the winter sleeping

melting pot (MELT-ing paht): where different types of people live together

metropolitan (met-ruh-PAH-li-tuhn): having to do with a large city

migrating (MYE-grate-ing): moving from one area to another

settlement (SET-uhl-muhnt): a small group of houses where people live

tourists (TOOR-ists): people who visit a place for fun

Index

Show What You Know

1. Why are the Northeast and Metropolitan regions called the oldest regions in the United States?
2. What are some mountain ranges that run through these regions?
3. What sports are popular in winter in the Northeast and Metropolitan regions?
4. What are some foods grown in these regions?
5. Name four products made in these regions.

Websites to Visit

mrnussbaum.com/third-grade-social-studies
www.postcardsfrom.com
www.nps.gov/nero

Author

Nancy Kelly Allen lives in Kentucky with her husband and two canine writing assistants, Roxi and Jazi. The Appalachian Mountains surround her home. In spring, the trees burst with blooms of red, pink, and white. In summer, green paints the hills until autumn splashes a rainbow on the leaves. A cool winter spits snow and sparkles the land silvery white. As Nancy writes, she peeks out the window and enjoys the view.

Meet The Author!
www.meetREMauthors.com

www.rourkeeducationalmedia.com

PHOTO CREDITS: Cover: © Florin Vinti, Jonathan Lesage, Steve Greer Photography, Sean Pavone, Alberto Loyo; Title Page: © aimintang; Page 3: © Sarah Winter; Page 5: © 2G1R; Page 6: © Library of Congress; Page 7: © River North Photography, Oleg Albinsky; Page 9: © Library of Congress; Page 11: © dhughes9; Page 12: © ryasick; Page 13: © Bill Florence; Page 14: © Denis Tangney Jr.; Page 15: © Sean Pavone Photo; © Erick Schmeidl; Page 17: © Meyrl Dieter Germany; Page 18: © Jonathan Lesage; Page 19: © Ken Weidermann; Page 20: © kirin_photo; Page 21: © mchebby; Page 22: © Cappi Thompson; Page 23: © maridau; Page 24: © bikerlondon; Page 25: © littleny; Page 26: © dhughes9, Jiri Hera, John A. Anderson; Page 27: © Sean Pavone Photo, Ken Weidermann, Paul Giamou; Page 28: © Denis Tangney Jr., ryasick, JeninVa; Page 29: © Spirit of America, River North Photography

Edited by: Jill Sherman

Cover and Interior design by: Tara Raymo

Library of Congress PCN Data

Northeast and Metropolitan Regions / Nancy Allen
(United States Regions)
ISBN 978-1-62717-673-6 (hard cover)
ISBN 978-1-62717-795-5(soft cover)
ISBN 978-1-62717-912-6 (e-Book)
Library of Congress Control Number: 2014934381

Also Available as:

ROURKE'S

Printed in the United States of America, North Mankato, Minnesota